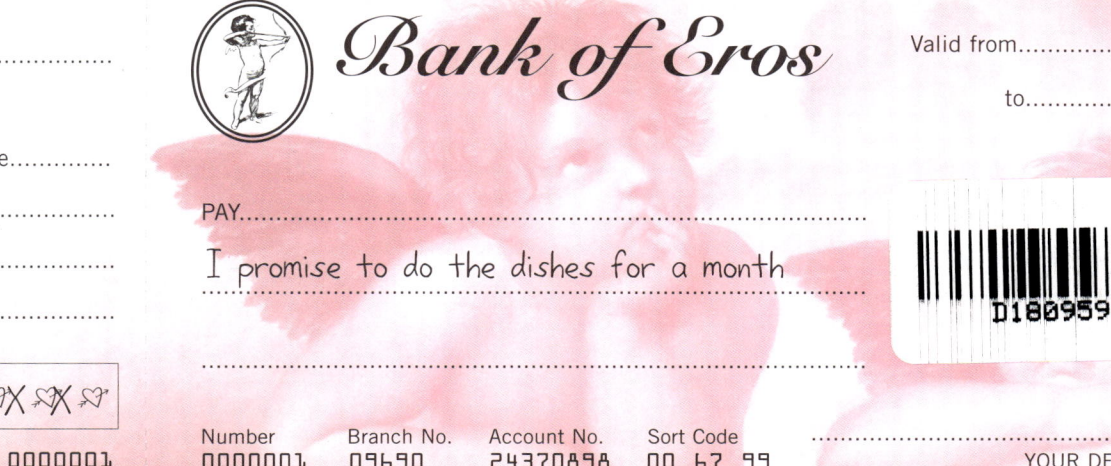

Date...............

Payee.............

....

....

....

X ✗X ✗X ✗

0000001

Bank of Eros

PAY..

I promise to do the dishes for a month

....

....

Valid from..................................

to.............................

D1809594

| Number | Branch No. | Account No. | Sort Code |
| 0000001 | 09690 | 24370898 | 00 67 99 |

....

YOUR DEVOTED LOVER

Date................

Payee.............

....

....

....

X ✘X ✘X ✘

0000002

Bank of Eros

PAY..

I promise to give you a back rub
....

....

Number	Branch No.	Account No.	Sort Code
0000002	0000002	09690	24370898	00 67 99

Valid from................................

to................................

X ✘X X ✘X ✘XX

....

YOUR DEVOTED LOVER

Date...............

Payee..............

....

....

....

X ♥ X ♥ X ♥

0000003

Bank of Eros

PAY...

I promise to bring you flowers every

Friday for a month

....

X ♥ X X ♥ X ♥ X ♥ X X

Valid from...............................

to...............................

Number	Branch No.	Account No.	Sort Code
0000003	09690	24370898	00 67 99

....

YOUR DEVOTED LOVER

Date...............

Payee..............

....

....

....

X ♥ X ♥ X ♥

0000004

Bank of Eros

Valid from................................

to................................

PAY..

I hereby agree to iron three of your shirts

X ♥ X X ♥ X ♥ X X

....

| Number | Branch No. | Account No. | Sort Code |
| 0000004 | 09690 | 24370898 | 00 67 99 |

....

YOUR DEVOTED LOVER

Date...............

Payee.............

....

....

....

X ♥X ♥X ♥

0000005

Bank of Eros

Valid from.................................

to.............................

PAY...

I owe you a romantic dinner in a

classy restaurant

X ♥X X ♥X ♥X X

Number	Branch No.	Account No.	Sort Code
0000005	09690	24370898	00 67 99

....

YOUR DEVOTED LOVER

Valid from.................................

to................................

Payee..............

....

....

....

Bank of Eros

PAY...

I promise to make you breakfast

in bed for a week

X ♡ X X ♡ X ♡ X X

X ♡ X ♡ X ♡

Number	Branch No.	Account No.	Sort Code
0000006	09690	24370898	00 67 99

0000006

YOUR DEVOTED LOVER

Date...............

Payee..............

....

....

....

X ♥ X ♥ X ♥

0000007

Bank of Eros

PAY...

I promise not to watch television during dinner

....

....

Number	Branch No.	Account No.	Sort Code
0000007	09690	24370898	00 67 99

Valid from...............................

to...............................

X ♥ X X ♥ X ♥ X X

....

YOUR DEVOTED LOVER

Date................

Payee..............

....

....

....

X ♡ X ♡ X

0000008

Bank of Eros

PAY...

I promise not to watch sports all weekend

....

X ♡ X X ♡ X ♡ X X

Valid from..................................

to..................................

Number	Branch No.	Account No.	Sort Code
0000008	09690	24370898	00 67 99

....

YOUR DEVOTED LOVER

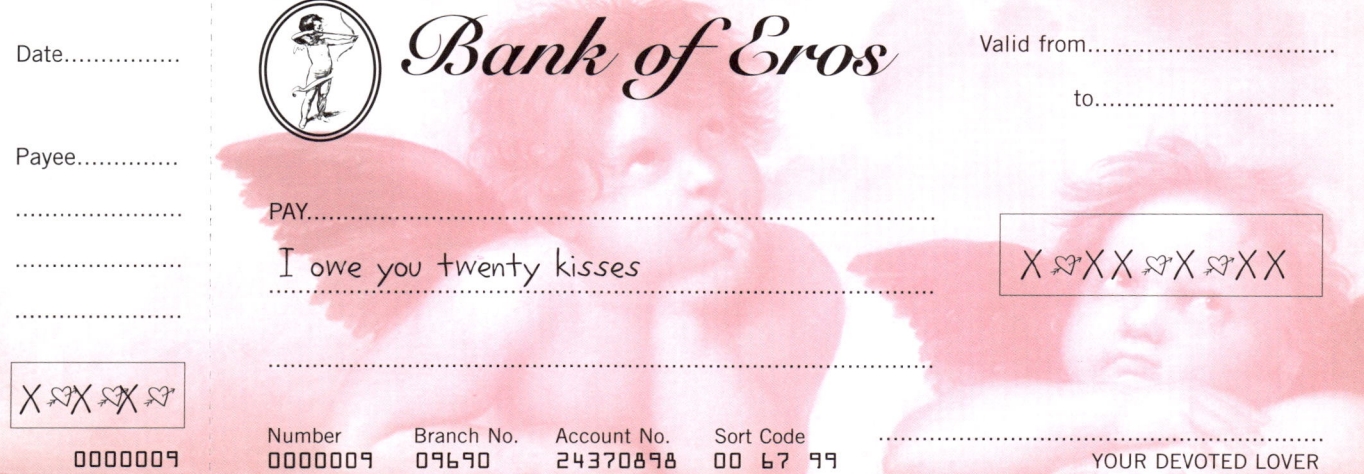

Date................

Payee..............

....

....

....

X ❤X ❤X ❤

0000009

Bank of Eros

PAY...

I owe you twenty kisses

X ❤X X ❤X ❤X X

Valid from................................

to................................

| Number | Branch No. | Account No. | Sort Code |
| 0000009 | 09690 | 24370898 | 00 67 99 |

....

YOUR DEVOTED LOVER

Date................

Bank of Eros

Valid from..................................

to..............................

Payee..............

....

....

....

PAY..

I owe you four "I love yous"

X 💘 X X 💘 X 💘 X X

X 💘 X 💘 X 💘

Number	Branch No.	Account No.	Sort Code
0000010	0000010	09690	24370898	00 67 99

YOUR DEVOTED LOVER

Date................

Payee.............

....

....

....

X ❤X ❤X ❤

0000011

Bank of Eros

PAY..

I agree to do the laundry without complaining

....

....

Number	Branch No.	Account No.	Sort Code
0000011	09690	24370898	00 67 99

Valid from................................

to................................

X ❤X X ❤X ❤X X

....

YOUR DEVOTED LOVER

Date................

Bank of Eros

Valid from....................................

to................................

Payee..............

....

....

....

PAY..

I promise to go shopping with you without

raising a single objection

X ♥ X X ♥ X ♥ X X

X ♥ X ♥ X ♥

0000012

Number
0000012

Branch No.
09690

Account No.
24370898

Sort Code
00 67 99

....

YOUR DEVOTED LOVER

Date...............

Payee..............

....

....

....

X ♥ X ♥ X ♥

0000013

Bank of Eros

PAY..

I promise to take you to the restaurant

of your choice
....

Valid from....................................

to................................

X ♥ X X ♥ X ♥ X X

| Number | Branch No. | Account No. | Sort Code |
| 0000013 | 09690 | 24370898 | 00 67 99 |

....

YOUR DEVOTED LOVER

Date...............

Payee..............

....

....

....

X ✍X ✍X ✍

0000014

Bank of Eros

PAY..

I promise to take you away for a

romantic weekend
....

Valid from.................................

to.................................

X ✍X X ✍X ✍X X

Number   Branch No.   Account No.   Sort Code
0000014   09690   24370898   00 67 99

....
YOUR DEVOTED LOVER

Date...............

Payee..............

....

....

....

X ❤X ❤X ❤

0000015

Bank of Eros

PAY...

I promise to make you the best dinner ever

....

Number	Branch No.	Account No.	Sort Code
0000015	09690	24370898	00 67 99

Valid from................................

to................................

X ❤X X ❤X ❤X X

....

YOUR DEVOTED LOVER

Date...............

Payee.............

....

....

....

X 💕X 💕X 💕

0000016

Bank of Eros

Valid from...................................

to...............................

PAY...

I promise to remember our anniversary

....

....

X 💕X X 💕X 💕X X

| Number | Branch No. | Account No. | Sort Code |
| 0000016 | 09690 | 24370898 | 00 67 99 |

YOUR DEVOTED LOVER

Date...............

Payee..............

....

....

....

X ♥X ♥X ♥♥

0000017

Bank of Eros

Valid from.................................

to...............................

PAY...

I promise not to leave the toilet seat up

....

....

X ♥XX ♥X ♥XX

Number	Branch No.	Account No.	Sort Code	
0000017	09690	24370898	00 67 99	YOUR DEVOTED LOVER

Date...............

Payee..............

....

....

....

X ❤X ❤X ❤

0000018

Bank of Eros

PAY..

I owe you a foot massage

....

....

Valid from.................................

to...............................

X ❤X X ❤X ❤X X

Number	Branch No.	Account No.	Sort Code
0000018	09690	24370898	00 67 99

....

YOUR DEVOTED LOVER

Date...............

Payee.............

....

....

....

X ✕X ✕X ✕

0000019

Bank of Eros

PAY...

I hereby agree to wash the car every

weekend for a month
....

Valid from...............................

to...............................

X ✕X X ✕X ✕X X

Number	Branch No.	Account No.	Sort Code
0000019	09690	24370898	00 67 99

....
YOUR DEVOTED LOVER

Bank of Eros

Valid from.................................

to................................

Payee..............

....

....

....

X ♥ X ♥ X ♥

0000020

PAY...

I promise not to leave wet towels all over

the bathroom floor

X ♥ X X ♥ X ♥ X X

Number	Branch No.	Account No.	Sort Code	
0000020	09690	24370898	00 67 99	

....

YOUR DEVOTED LOVER

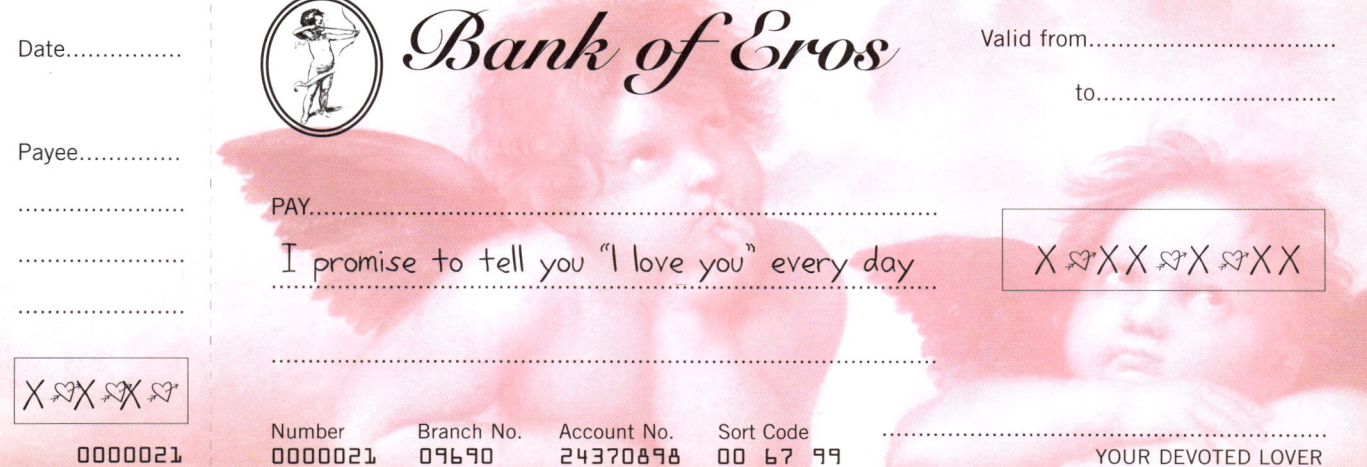

Date...............

Payee..............

....

....

....

X ✗X ✗X ✗

0000021

Bank of Eros

Valid from.................................

to.............................

PAY...

I promise to tell you "I love you" every day

....

....

X ✗X X ✗X ✗X X

Number   Branch No.   Account No.   Sort Code
0000021   09690   24370898   00 67 99

....
YOUR DEVOTED LOVER

Date................

Payee..............

....

....

....

X ❤X ❤X ❤

0000022

Bank of Eros

PAY..

I promise to run a hot bath for you

when you are tired

Valid from...................................

to.................................

X ❤X X ❤X ❤X X

Number	Branch No.	Account No.	Sort Code
0000022	09690	24370898	00 67 99

....

YOUR DEVOTED LOVER

Date...............

Payee..............

....

....

....

X 💘 X 💘 X 💘

0000023

Bank of Eros

PAY..

I promise to call if I will be home late

....

Valid from.................................

to.................................

X 💘 X X 💘 X 💘 X X

Number	Branch No.	Account No.	Sort Code
0000023	09690	24370898	00 67 99

....

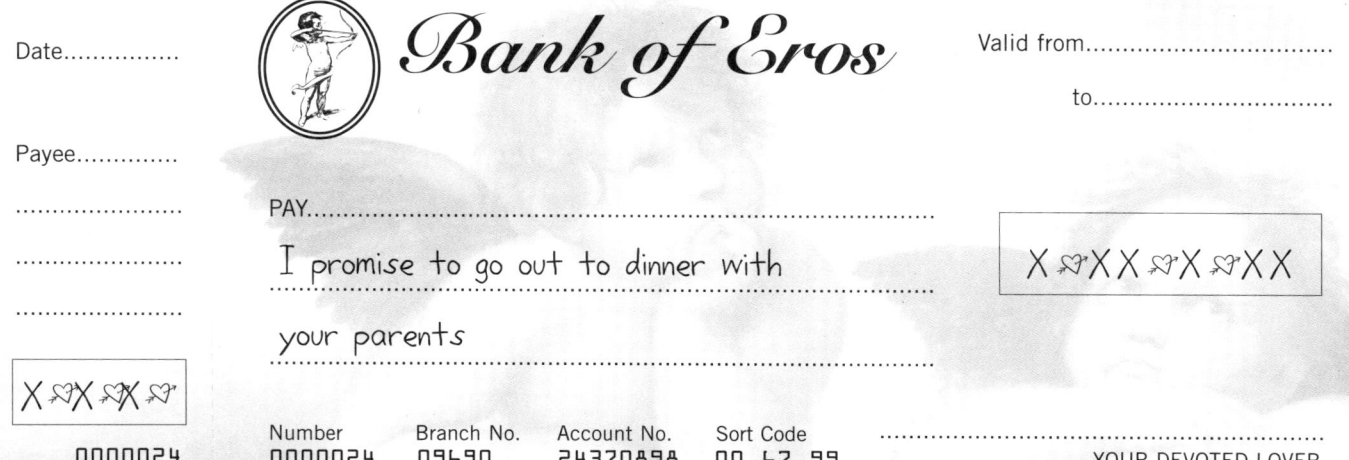

Date.................

Payee..............

....

....

....

X ♥X ♥X ♥

0000024

Bank of Eros

PAY...

I promise to go out to dinner with

your parents

Number   Branch No.   Account No.   Sort Code
0000024   09690   24370898   00 67 99

Valid from.................................

to...............................

X ♥X X ♥X ♥X X

....
YOUR DEVOTED LOVER

Date...............

Payee.............

....

....

....

X ♥X X♥ ♥

0000025

Bank of Eros

PAY..

I owe you a quiet evening of cuddling

on the couch

....

| Number | Branch No. | Account No. | Sort Code |
| 0000025 | 09690 | 24370898 | 00 67 99 |

Valid from...................................

to..............................

X ♥X X ♥X ♥X X

....
YOUR DEVOTED LOVER

Date................

Payee..............

....

....

....

X ♥ X ♥ X ♥

0000026

Bank of Eros

PAY...

I promise to tell you how good you look

every day

....

Number	Branch No.	Account No.	Sort Code
0000026	09690	24370898	00 67 99

Valid from...................................

to..................................

X ♥ X X ♥ X ♥ X X

....
YOUR DEVOTED LOVER

Date...............

Payee..............

....

....

....

X ⚭X ⚭X ⚭

0000027

Bank of Eros

PAY...

I hereby agree to act happy when we

go out with your friends

Valid from.....................................

to.....................................

X ⚭X X ⚭X ⚭X X

Number	Branch No.	Account No.	Sort Code
0000027	0000027	09690	24370898	00 67 99

....

YOUR DEVOTED LOVER

Date...............

Payee..............

....

....

....

X ♡X ♡X ♡

0000028

Bank of Eros

Valid from................................

to................................

PAY..

I promise to help put away the groceries
....

....

X ♡ X X ♡ X ♡ X X

Number	Branch No.	Account No.	Sort Code
0000028	09690	24370898	00 67 99

....

YOUR DEVOTED LOVER

Date...............

Payee..............

....

....

....

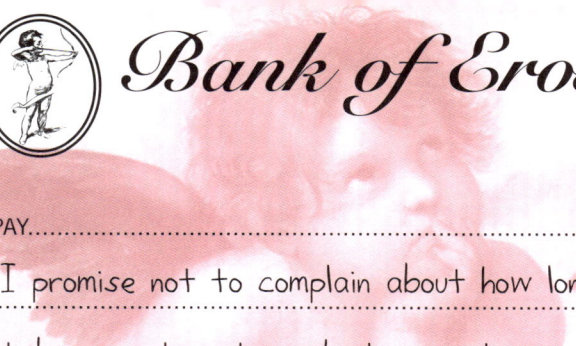

Bank of Eros

Valid from.................................

to.................................

PAY...

I promise not to complain about how long it

....

takes you to get ready to go out

....

X ✗ X X ✗ X ✗ X X

X ✗ X ✗ X ✗

0000029

Number	Branch No.	Account No.	Sort Code
0000029	09690	24370898	00 67 99

....

YOUR DEVOTED LOVER

Date...............

Payee.............

....

....

....

X ❤ X ❤ X ❤

0000030

Bank of Eros

PAY...

I promise not to fall asleep in front

of the television
....

Valid from...................................

to................................

X ❤ X X ❤ X ❤ X X

Number	Branch No.	Account No.	Sort Code
0000030	09690	24370898	00 67 99

....

YOUR DEVOTED LOVER

Date...............

Payee..............

....

....

....

X ♥X ☜X ☜

0000031

Bank of Eros

PAY...

....

....

Number	Branch No.	Account No.	Sort Code
0000031	09690	24370898	00 67 99

Valid from...............................

to...............................

X ☜XX ☜X ☜X ☜XX

....

YOUR DEVOTED LOVER

Date...............

Payee.............

....

....

....

X ♥X ♥X ♥

0000032

Bank of Eros

Valid from..................................

to...............................

PAY..

....

....

X ♥X X ♥X X ♥X X

Number	Branch No.	Account No.	Sort Code
0000032	09690	24370898	00 67 99

....
YOUR DEVOTED LOVER

Date...............

Payee.............

....

....

....

X ♡ X ♡ X ♡

0000033

Bank of Eros

PAY...

....

....

| Number | Branch No. | Account No. | Sort Code |
| 0000033 | 09690 | 24370898 | 00 67 99 |

Valid from.................................

to.................................

X ♡ X X ♡ X ♡ X X

....

YOUR DEVOTED LOVER

Date...............

Payee..............

....

....

....

X ♡ X ♡ X ♡

0000034

Bank of Eros

PAY...

....

....

Number	Branch No.	Account No.	Sort Code
0000034	09690	24370898	00 67 99

Valid from.................................

to................................

X ♡ X X ♡ X ♡ X X

....
YOUR DEVOTED LOVER

Date................

Payee..............

....

....

....

X ♥ X ♥ X ♥

0000035

Bank of Eros

PAY...

....

....

X ♥ X X ♥ X ♥ X X

Valid from................................

to................................

Number	Branch No.	Account No.	Sort Code
0000035	09690	24370898	00 67 99

....

YOUR DEVOTED LOVER

Date.................

Payee.............

....

....

....

X ♡ X ♡ X ♡

0000036

Bank of Eros

PAY...

....

....

X ♡ X X ♡ X ♡ X X

Valid from...................................

to..............................

Number	Branch No.	Account No.	Sort Code
0000036	09690	24370898	00 67 99

....

YOUR DEVOTED LOVER